Brian
Vanden
Brink's

At Home

by the sea

HOUSES DESIGNED FOR LIVING AT THE WATER'S EDGE

PHOTOGRAPHY BY BRIAN VANDEN BRINK ■ **TEXT BY BRUCE SNIDER**

ISBN: 978-0-89272-754-4

Design by Chilton Creative
Printed in China

5   4   3   2   1

Down East
Books · Magazine · Online
Camden, Maine
Book orders: 1-800-685-7962
www.downeast.com
Distributed to the trade by National Book Network, Inc.

Library of Congress Cataloging-in-Publication Data

Vanden Brink, Brian, 1951-
  At home by the sea : houses designed for living at the water's edge /
photography by Brian Vanden Brink ; text by Bruce Snider. -- 1st ed.
    p. cm.
  ISBN 978-0-89272-754-4 (trade hardcover : alk. paper)
  1. Seaside architecture--United States. 2. Architecture, Domestic--
United States. I. Snider, Bruce, 1958- II. Title.

NA7575.V36 2008
728.0914'6--dc22
                        2007041853

To my mother and my sisters, whose keen eyes have always challenged me to sharpen my own. To my father, who first taught me how to get a job done. To my sons, Ari, Jesse, and Daniel, who fill our home by the sea with life and laughter. To my wife, Liz, who makes all things possible.

—Bruce Snider

To my mother, Lena Vanden Brink (1915–2007), whose passing brings sadness and reminds me of the fleeting nature of all mankind. To my father, Gordon Vanden Brink (1917–   ), a World War II hero, even at this moment dying of cancer, showing me courage and faith as he faces the end of his days. To my grandson, Ezra, whom I love, a beautiful reminder of the newness and joy of life itself.

—Brian Vanden Brink

Contents

Acknowledgements 6

Photographer's Statement 8

Introduction 11

Koehler House   *Bay of Fundy, Canada* 19

Island Retreat   *Coastal Maine* 29

Summer Cottage   *Sorrento, Maine* 39

Deer Isle House   *Deer Isle, Maine* 49

Summer House   *North Haven, Maine* 56

Burns/Spaulding House   *Georgetown, Maine* 65

Cameron Camp   *Southport Island, Maine* 75

Cavalli Beach House   *Biddeford Pool, Maine* 82

Nolen/Denny Vacation House   *Cape Cod, Massachusetts* 93

Harper's Island House *Chatham, Massachusetts* 101

Roach House *Nantucket, Massachusetts* 110

Jeffers House *Martha's Vineyard* 119

Two Cottages *Martha's Vineyard* 128

Writer's Cottage *Martha's Vineyard* 145

Vacation House *Rhode Island* 149

McKenna House *Hilton Head, South Carolina* 158

Caribbean Vacation House *St. Barthelemy* 167

Roosevelt House *St. Barthelemy* 175

Robertson House *Belvedere, California* 183

James House *Carmel, California* 191

Architectural Resources 200

Acknowledgments

My involvement in this book began, in a way, more than 25 years ago. Fresh out of college and in the midst of a severe recession, I had had the outlandish luck of finding work with an architectural firm in the coastal village of Rockport, Maine. An architectural photographer rented studio space in the same building, and when I needed a break I would often wander across the hall to see if he had shot anything interesting. Brian Vanden Brink was only a few years older than I, but he had already achieved an obvious mastery of his craft. And because he was as much in love with architecture as I was, we had plenty to talk about. "Wait till you see this one," he would say, handing me another gorgeous 4x5 transparency, another window into a small, perfect world.

Some years later, when my work shifted primarily to magazine writing, I encountered Brian's work again. By then he had established himself in the very top rank of his profession, and his standing among architects would make his lens the conduit for just the sort of houses I wanted to write about. So I happily resumed my visits to Brian's studio, which continue to this day. I now arrive with an agenda—scouting houses for publication—but our visits remain essentially as they were in the old days. We pore through Brian's photographs the way my sons study each other's baseball cards.

The object of our study is residential architecture, and the effort would go nowhere without the architects and builders whose creativity makes this an endlessly rewarding pursuit, or without the owners, whose resources and inspiration make the buildings possible and whose generosity makes them available to the world. I believe I speak for Brian as well when I say that they have supplied far more than the raw material for our own work. Over the years, sharing our thoughts about each house, we have also shared our evolving philosophies of architecture and of life.

I welcomed the opportunity to collaborate with Brian on a book of great waterfront houses as a natural extension of our long-standing friendship. In these pages, Brian expresses his view of architecture with the polished eloquence of his visuals, while I work mine out in words. Underlying both is the undiminished excitement we feel at the sight of something new and wonderful. Each of us, in his own way, is saying, "Wait till you see this one."

—Bruce Snider

I want to take this opportunity to recognize the work of many people, without whom this book would not exist. First of all, I want to thank Bruce Snider for doing such a diligent job of research and writing for this book. I have known Bruce for many years and he was a natural choice when the time came to select our writer. His knowledge of architecture and skill with words are exceptional. I appreciate that he is conversant in so many different architectural styles and periods. He's done a great job. I also want to thank the editors at Down East Books for asking me to do this book with them. They are such good people to work with that I couldn't turn it down. Thanks, Neale Sweet, John Viehman, and Michael Steere. Lynda Chilton, as usual, was an angel to work with as designer for the book. Thanks, Lynda for your patience with me during those many changes and revisions.

These houses were all shot on assignment, either for architects, designers or magazines. The work of these architects is outstanding and I am honored to be able to work for them. Not only have they proven themselves to be highly professional and creative, but as people, they have been so good to work with. Doing a shoot is hard work. It takes a lot of patience, long hours and just plain physical labor. Almost all of these house shoots had at least one person present and involved from the architect's office, usually more than

that. On assignments for magazines, the editors who have been present have been wonderful and fun people who have made the hard work so much easier. In every case, those who have been on the shoot have worked so hard and really made it possible to get the shots you will see on the pages of this book. I can't do this type of shooting by myself. I'm very grateful to all who have done heavy lifting to make these shots possible.

I especially want to thank my assistants who spend so much time with me, not only on location but in the office as well. They really make things happen and are invaluable partners in this work. I specifically want to mention Jason Crain and Todd Caverly, who assisted me during most of these assignments. They are good men and good friends.

I want to thank my friends Bill Komulainen, Gary Bailey and Jim Yesberger who help me keep my feet on the ground and my heart in the right place.

I am so thankful for my daughter Maegan, my son-in-law Troy, and our grandson Ezra. They are always a source of encouragement and joy to us. Finally, I want to thank my wife, Kathleen, who is my best friend and faithful life partner. She is truly a great woman and a deep soul. I'm blessed that she stays with me and helps me keep balance and perspective. Life is good, thank the good Lord.

—Brian Vanden Brink

Photographer's Statement

Growing up in Omaha, Nebraska, I lived near the sea. No, not the sea one might usually think of, but an inland sea; a sea of grass with waves of rolling hills and unbroken horizons. I didn't learn much about boats, but I knew about the "prairie schooners" that brought pioneers to the great plains in the 1800s. I loved going out for long drives into the real prairie of western Nebraska, exploring and photographing in those remote areas, and that's about as close as I ever came to sailing. For as long as I can remember, I've loved the vastness and emptiness of that landscape. The writer and photographer Wright Morris spent his early years in Nebraska and once wrote that "the plains conditioned what I see and what I find in the world to write about." He also said that "the plain is a metaphysical landscape...where there is almost nothing to see, there man sees the most." I think I know what he meant. At least I know that's how I felt about the prairies and how I feel now when I am near the ocean. When Kathleen and I left Nebraska in 1976, I knew we were headed for the sea. I knew I would need to be near that open horizon and feel that "emptiness" I had felt on the plains of Nebraska, where fences were few and far between and it seemed you could just sail away.

I began to learn photography as a twenty-something young man, after borrowing my dad's 35mm camera and finding that I actually understood (kind of)

what was going on. It made sense to me and I was immediately fascinated, wanting to learn more. I read everything I could on the subject and shot LOTS of film, making many mistakes, and trying to figure out what I'd done wrong. I also spent a lot of time looking at the work of photographers and artists whose work I responded to and found emotionally engaging. Edward Weston, Walker Evans, Ansel Adams, Charles Scheeler, Edward Hopper, Giorgio DeChirico, and many others helped me learn about composition, style, and light. Soon, I bought my first large format view camera (a 4x5 inch Crown Graphic) which needed to be tripod mounted and framed and focused with a cloth over my head. The slower and more deliberate pace of working with a view camera was a good fit for me and I began to work very much as I do today, more than thirty years later.

I still shoot film (transparencies), working with a Sinar 4x5 view camera mounted on a tripod. I have a large selection of lenses as well as a 120 mm Pentax roll film camera that I sometimes use when I can't fit the 4x5 into a tight spot or the shot can only be hand held. I'm not a "technical" kind of photographer. I'm not into gadgets or equipment. I don't own a light meter, color meter, or many other tools that are available. My lighting equipment is very simple and I try to use it infrequently, relying more and more on reflectors to fill in shadows. I believe that developing the eye for seeing and having an awareness of light are the most important tools a photographer brings to a shoot.

I learned photography by working with hard, clear light that produces crisp shadows and reveals form and texture. I still like that kind of light and I believe that if people feel anything when they look at my work, perhaps the most basic and important element they are responding to is the light. I try to work with "available light"—the light that already exists in a space—and try to avoid getting into complicated lighting scenarios. My feeling is that God illuminates things best so I try to work with the light I've been given. I rely heavily on the sun and the way it defines a building, and I work in rhythm with the sun as the day passes. This means I must work quickly and anticipate when the light will be right in a given area so that I can have the shot ready to go when the conditions are best.

When I began taking photographs, my subjects were grain elevators, farm structures, fuel storage tanks, abandoned buildings, and, of course, their relationship to that "oceanic" landscape. Today I work with architects, landscape architects, interior designers, and publishers doing much the same thing, but now the buildings are very different and more sophisticated. The palette I worked with for this book however, is not all that different and, like Wright Morris, my perspective has been conditioned by what I saw and experienced as a young man growing up in the Midwest. I still love to show buildings in their landscape, especially when the landscape has an endless horizon. So when Down East approached me about doing the next book in the *At Home* series, it was a natural and easy decision to do a book on seaside houses.

I don't like talking about or trying to explain my work, but simply put, I believe my job is to record, interpret, and present the work of others in the most favorable way . It seems to me to be much more a collaboration than a solo performance. God makes the light and the landscape. Architects and designers create the buildings I am assigned to shoot. Ultimately, my job is just to make sure that I am in the right place at the right time and to get the shot. I know that I am very fortunate to have work that I love even after thirty years. I also have the privilege of working with some of the best architects, designers, and editors in the business. But having said all this, I realize that I'm a picture guy and, as Edward Hopper once said, "If I could say it in words, I wouldn't need to paint..." Hope you enjoy the book.

Brian Vanden Brink
Camden, Maine
2007

Introduction

At Home by the Sea

The sun reflects off the rippling surface of the sea, spreading a shifting quilt of light across the ceiling. A salty breeze stirs the curtains. Framed in the window, a small boat rides quietly at her mooring. Children wander along the shore, turning over rocks, looking for crabs.

The appeal of living within sight of salt water runs deep, and it has a long history. Some two thousand years ago, Julius Caesar and other members of the Roman elite kept luxurious villas in Stabiae, a resort town overlooking the Bay of Naples. When Europeans first waded ashore in North America, the coastline was dotted with seasonal Indian settlements, whose shell mounds bore witness to centuries of use.

But while Native Americans may well have enjoyed the seaside for its own sake, they came also for the bounty of resources that the sea provided. And long after Europeans came to control the continent, the American coastline would remain the province of commerce: fishing, trade, shipbuilding, and dozens of other related enterprises. At the height of the whaling industry, near the turn of the 19th century, the island of Nantucket was home to some 10,000 people. Few of

them, it is safe to say, were there for the scenery. Those who lived by the sea were those who drew their living from it. Any enjoyment they derived from their saltwater views must have been tempered by an experience of the sea as a place of arduous toil, a killer of sailors, and the mother of storms. The houses they built reflect the practical considerations of survival in an often harsh environment.

As early as the mid 18th century, southern plantation owners were sailing annually to New England to escape the summer heat in shorefront mansions. But appreciation of the shore for its own sake would not take hold among Americans until a century later, when Gilded Age industrialists pioneered the concept of vacation. Following the lead of artists and "rusticators," who extolled the aesthetic qualities of the coast and romanticized those who labored in its traditional industries, the robber barons built palatial getaways in such enclaves as Newport, Rhode Island, and Bar Harbor, Maine. These "cottages," geared toward leisure pursuits and reflecting the gentler moods of the sea, have influenced the design of shorefront homes ever since.

Expanded rail and steamship service and a growing middle class would soon bring Americans of more modest means to the shore, where they boarded in farmhouses and, as tourism emerged as an industry, rental cottages, hotels, and resorts. Unaccustomed to leisure, they came tentatively at first. Some of the earliest summer resorts, such as Oak Bluffs, on the Massachusetts island of Martha's Vineyard, and Ocean Grove, New Jersey, began as "camp meeting" tent colonies. There, congregants sought spiritual renewal and—perhaps not incidentally—the freedom of the rural landscape and the bracing proximity of salt water. Over the years, religious tent colonies gave way to vacation communities and a casual breed of shorefront home that typically provided just enough shelter for summer use. In a common scenario, mothers and children took up residence for the season while fathers commuted to jobs in the city.

The post-World War II explosion in prosperity, mobility, and leisure time delivered more visitors and residents to the coast. Affordable air travel brought

more of the country's shoreline—and offshore locations like the Caribbean islands—within reach of its population centers. Today, a revolution in telecommunications coincides with a large and wealthy generation's arrival at retirement age, releasing an unprecedented wave of Americans to live wherever they choose. More of them than ever before are choosing to live by the sea.

The results have been mixed for waterfront communities. The migration to the shore brings new blood and commercial vitality but also inflates property values, forcing out families that for generations have relied upon the sea—and on waterfront access—for their livelihood. The escalation in coastal property values has driven a parallel increase in the resources devot-

ed to the construction of waterfront houses. The outcomes include some of the most architecturally interesting examples ever built and many more that are undistinguished in every way except their size and the amount of shorefront land they divert from other uses. It seems likely that the coastal scene will gain no new saltwater farms, rows of modestly handsome houses for fish-plant workers, or rough but charming seasonal cottages. The owner of one fine example of the latter, which stands on land now worth many times its market value as a structure, said, "I'm sure if we sold it, it would be torn down immediately."

But that cottage survives, as do the countless other anonymous but noteworthy structures that constitute our coastal architectural heritage: saltwater farmhouses in Greek Revival white, the austere homes of Nantucket's Quaker whaling captains, fishing shacks built of whatever materials were at hand, Carpenter Gothic summer cottages that speak of the moral-uplift mission of early vacationers, grand Shingle Style cot-

tages that served the urban elite in a "casual" style (but nevertheless required a staff of servants), glass-walled Modernist houses that reflect the contemporary taste for immersion in nature.

Our interest in these buildings is more than historical. Every building responds to its site, and the coastal environment seems as salutary for houses as it has long been reputed to be for people. The old ones, built when living by the shore meant working by the shore, have an austere purposefulness that reflects both the character of their first inhabitants and the inevitability of coastal storms. The simple "camps" that appeared around the turn of the 20th century are as effective as ever at reconnecting harried urbanites with the rhythms of nature. For a century and a half this front-row perch has also been a showplace for the work of the country's best residential architects. Henry Hobson Richardson developed the Shingle Style for this setting, with repercussions that echo to this day. Contemporary architects test their mettle with houses that rise to the level of art while withstanding the rigors of exposed coastal sites: sun and salt atmosphere, storms that drive rain vertically up the face of a wall, windblown sand that can etch window glass. The combination of such challenges with the ever-changing, always compelling backdrop of the sea makes successful shorefront houses a very special breed.

The houses on the following pages make that point emphatically. Ranging in geography from New Brunswick to northern California, they comprise a selective cross-section of coastal architectural traditions. Including year-round family homes, vacation getaways, and retirement dwellings, they span a wide variety of approaches to building on the coast. But while they differ in region, era, style, and materials, each reflects in every aspect the purpose of living fully at the edge of the land. New or old, humble or grand, each is at home by the sea.

Koehler House

Bay of Fundy, Canada
Julie Snow Architects

A mile of undisturbed granite shoreline on Canada's Bay of Fundy calls for something very special in any house that would occupy it. But this vacation residence does not presume to compete with the primordial grandeur of its site. Its minimalist structure projects no peaked roof into the sky. Its forms embody no biomorphic symmetry, no archetypal markers of house or home. Its horizontal planes follow the contours of the land, stepping down-slope toward the shore. Like the earth on which it perches, scoured to bare rock, the building shows its bones: floors to stand on, a roof overhead, and glass walls to fend off the wind. "It's not warm and cuddly," says owner Mary Beth Koehler. She and her husband, David, whose year-round home is in

Minneapolis, bought this land and built on its seaward-most point because, she says, "We really wanted to embrace the vastness of the ocean." They would be traveling a long way to visit this shoreline, and they intended to experience it as fully as possible.

Architect Julie Snow took them at their word. "Everything takes place within the presence of this rocky site," says Snow of the house she designed. "It's almost like camping or being on a boat." The Koehlers are art collectors, but here "There is no space for art collections, or any reminder of their life everywhere else in the world. It's about disconnecting and being in this place in a very particular way." At every turn, the house reminds you of where you are, primarily by means of its transparent shell. But Snow took the matter further, seasoning the plan with what she calls "little inconveniences" that intensify one's experience of

Opposite—Two islands house all the functions of a simple kitchen, leaving perimeter walls open to the view. Left—A bluestone chimney mass seems to rise from the bedrock of the shore.

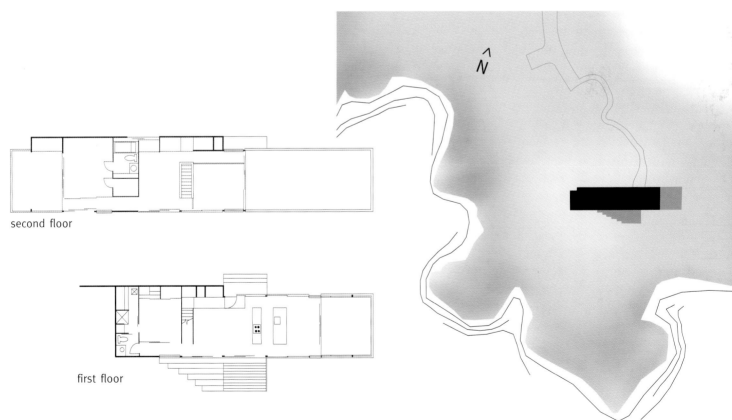

second floor

first floor

place. The internal stair forces a switchback path from floor to floor, she points out, "So, as you rise up through the walls of the stairs, you're facing an uninterrupted horizon view." The kitchen consists of two islands floating in the middle of a glass-walled space. With no wall cabinets—and no walls, for that matter—cooking is "like being out on a deck working at a table. There is nothing between you and that site."

In addition to its magnificent shoreline, the Koehlers' property includes acre upon acre of forest, bogs, and rock outcrops. "Perfect moose country," Koehler calls it. "Total wilderness land, which has been a challenge. We had to have a road put in before we could even see it." Beyond that, she says, "We hardly disturbed the landscape at all; it's just natural." And far from tamed. "It's trying to take over. We don't have any

Top—A set of sliding panels, withdrawn in this photograph, open the master bedroom to a glass-walled corridor. Above—Like every aspect of the building, this covered porch at the lower level imposes as little structure as possible between its owners and the visual environment. Opposite—The building's stepped massing follows the contours of it sloping site.

Right—The simple geometry and unbroken planes of the interior create a quiet contrast with the rugged scenery outside. Above— Details draw on the minimalist repertoire of mid-century Modernism.

yard, but we've found we have to work just to keep the wilderness at bay. We spend a lot of time just cutting back the wilderness." For relief, the nearby town of St. Andrews offers the company of friends and the occasional dose of civilization, though in an appealingly subdued form. "It's like turning the clock back fifty years," Koehler says. "It's very peaceful, unpretentious, not ridden with commercialism." Even a town of seventeen hundred people must seem metropolitan, though, when one comes home to the exposure and solitude of this shore. "People near us thought we were crazy to build way out there on the ocean," says Koehler. And maybe so, she allows, having weathered storms with hundred-mile-per-hour winds and blinding, horizontal rain. "But it's glorious. For me it is just an adventure to have a house like this."

Top left—The stair from the first floor presents this deliberately framed view. Above and opposite—The building's abstract form, which offers no traditional cues of house or home, perfectly reflects the spirit of this solitary place.

Island Retreat

Coastal Maine

Lance Grindle, builder/designer

Lance Grindle did his best not to build this house. When the owner approached the Mt. Desert Island, Maine, builder with his notion of a retreat on a smaller, nearby island, the builder made his disinterest plain. "I told him I had no desire to go out to the end of the earth," he says, "because I had plenty of work on this island." When the fellow persisted, Grindle thought he would put the matter to rest by simply ask-

ing for way too much money. But the owner called his bluff. More than twenty years—and one extraordinary building—later, it is impossible to say which man got the better of the deal.

Then, as now, this island was a remote outpost. "Fishing is the only industry," the builder says, "and at that point in time there were forty-eight adults and children." Make that forty-nine. A spotty ferry sched-

Set on 11 acres of manicured grounds, this island retreat blends architectural influences from Japan, the Pacific Northwest, and Down East Maine.

Clad in weather-resistant red cedar, Douglas fir, and mahogany, the building has bleached to a uniform driftwood gray. Even exposed to the storms of the North Atlantic, these materials will stand up well without the protection of paint.

ule made commuting impossible, so the builder became an islander for the duration of the job. "The crews could only come in the summer, when the sailing is good. In the fall, when the seas got rough, everyone would go away, and I would stay and patiently work through the winter." His client made sure he never got bored. "He wanted the building to last at least two hundred years without significant maintenance," Grindle says. "He didn't want to see any sheetrock, aluminum, plastic, etc., etc." With no architect's plans to work

from, builder and owner hashed out the design inch by inch. "I actually did mockups of various aspects for his approval."

The building that emerged is deceptively understated. "It's pretty basic," The builder says. "There's not a lot of jogs and wings. He was very enamored of Japanese design, and simplicity." That influence is evident in the temple-grounds landscaping, the broad, flaring roof, and the way the building seems to hover above the ground. Closer inspection reveals an intensity of craftsmanship

Island Retreat 31

more common to the boatyard than to the construction site. Woodworker Joe Tracy contributed custom furniture and cabinetry, rice-paper doors, and the birch-bark panels that line the living room's upper walls. Stonemason Jeff Gammelin stacked up a massive stone fireplace with nearly invisible mortar joints. The building's exposed roof beams are quarter-sawn Douglas fir; the wall paneling, mahogany. "We used yacht-type joinery," Grindle says, down to the sub-sills, which he assembled with keyed lap joints. The concrete footings—mixed and poured by hand, because the ferry would not float a mixer truck—are reinforced with bronze rod, rather than steel.

In obsessive attention to detail, it seems, the owner had found the perfect partner. "He wanted overhead can lights, but he didn't want to see them," says the

Opposite—Dark, recessed mortar joints give the stone masonry a dry-laid appearance. Left—The kitchen's cotton ceiling panels conceal recessed lighting fixtures. Below—Every interior door bears a unique design in mahogany and rice paper.

builder, who hid the fixtures behind a ceiling of cotton panels framed with narrow strips of fir. "He didn't want to see light switches," but some could not be hidden, "so I converted most of the visible ones to yacht-quality toggle switches, with tags under them saying what they operate." The shower has a domed ceiling, so water that condenses there will run down the walls rather than drip on one's head. Its teak floor grate is suspended above a copper pan, "so you can hear the water trickling down."

"In the end it was a two-and-a-half- to three-year commitment," Grindle says, "and I still have an open invitation to go out and address things." Not to fix mistakes, mind you, but to tweak and tune and improve, to resume what he calls "the constant search for perfection."

The hands that built the house also produced most of its furnishings. In this bedroom, the rice paper doors, birch bark wall paneling, and custom furniture and light fixtures all reflect the same artistic sensibility and craftsmanship.

Summer Cottage

Sorrento, Maine
Bernhard & Priestly Architecture

"**W**e don't want this to be 'correct.'" So declared the new owners of this summer cottage on Maine's Down East coast. Their rather formal year-round house in Richmond, Virginia, was suitable for their life in town, but summers in Maine called for something more casual. The cottage, originally built in the 1960s, supplied the crucial ingredient—a front-row seat at the rocky edge of Frenchman Bay, with island-dotted views of Hancock Point to the west and Mt. Desert Island to the south—but the building fell short of the site's extraordinary potential. The legally grandfathered location, only steps from the shore, came with a one-time chance to add a limited amount of square footage. But a relatively modest addition, along with a thorough exterior renovation and some beautifully integrated landscaping, made the most of that opportunity.

Opposite—The approach to this cottage leads visitors literally down the garden path. Above—A trellis and benches make the kitchen entry a tiny outdoor room.

The scene unfolds in a sequence of vignettes that begins as one approaches from a parking area, located a discreet distance from the building. A long entry path winds through dense plantings of native species and naturalized perennials that feather out into the surrounding spruce woodland. Beds of flowering plantings surround the house, erasing the line between landscape and architecture. Bedrock outcroppings segue to stone walking paths, dry-stone landscape walls, and masonry of local stone at the house's foundation and chimneys, further entwining site and structure. The cedar-shingled walls rise to an appealing jumble of roof shapes—gables, sheds, and dustpan dormers—that look as much grown as designed.

The cottage spreads out along the shore, but because it consists of three connected pavilions—a main building flanked by a master bedroom and the new guest quarters—it presents itself more as a gateway than a wall, the links between sections offering glimpses of the water beyond. The building's many offsets and recesses also create a series of semi-enclosed outdoor spaces that make the inland side of the house more than just walk-through space. The interior follows a similar approach, with human-scale rooms elaborated with built-in cabinets, bookcases, and seating recesses. A window seat with water views is within

Above—The master bedroom opens onto a private garden with a calming green and white palette. Opposite—The new guest quarters comprise a self-contained apartment that can be opened to the main house.

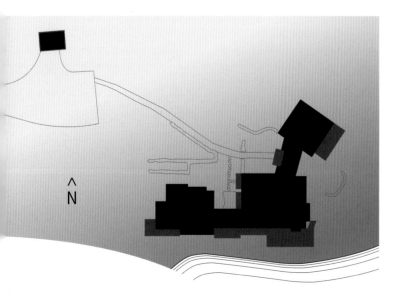

second floor

first floor

warming distance of the main room's stone fireplace. In the guests' sitting room, a U-shaped nook with a built-in bookcase invites reading or intimate conversation (convertible to a bed, it also doubles the suite's sleepover capacity).

Appealing as its indoor amenities are, however, the building directs attention foremost toward the sea. Every room except the baths takes in broad views of the water, and every ground-floor room opens onto an outdoor living space. Narrow by necessity—the cottage is that close to the shore—the long main deck includes two bays wide enough to accommodate groups. The master-bedroom deck, tucked into the trees, offers a

Left—Unfinished wood paneling and cabinetry maintain the casual atmosphere of the original building. Above—This window seat in the guest quarters is perfectly situated for reading, conversation, or contemplation of the garden outside.

Summer Cottage 45

more private spot. The guest-bedroom's vest-pocket porch, hidden from the rest of the house, is more secluded still. Each of these shoreline perches offers a slightly different prospect of salt water, islands, and sky. And like the other carefully composed scenes that make up this cottage, each is a natural stage set for enacting the rituals of summer; each strikes a slightly different note on the timeless theme of retreat. It takes a lot of work to make a building feel like a naturally occurring phenomenon, but none of that effort shows here. The result may not be correct, but it comes close to being perfectly right.

Above—The flower gardens that surround the cottage feather out into the natural woodland greenery. Above right—The master bedroom design conveys more than a hint of screened porch. Below right—The guest bedroom's deck offers privacy, with a view.

Deer Isle House

Deer Isle, Maine
Elliott Elliott Norelius Architecture

Deer Isle, where the waters of Maine's Penobscot and Blue Hill bays mix, is a pilgrimage site for East Coast sailors. That made this narrow point of land on the island's east shore both attractive and challenging to its current owners. "We had sailed up here a lot, starting probably thirty years ago," says the owner, who, with her husband, recently retired here from New York. The property offered a long south-facing shore on a sheltered inlet with deep water and a fine anchorage for their boat. It also came with a derelict gravel pit, brackish groundwater, and a very narrow area on which to build. But it was not the gravel pit or the mounds of earth piled up from its excavation that posed the greatest concern to these owners; it was the

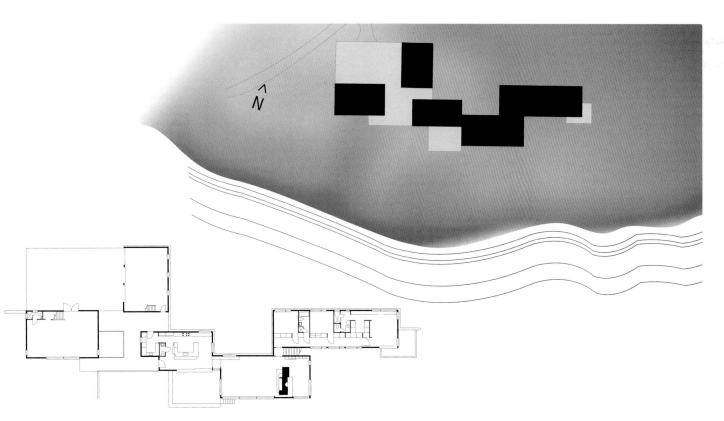

Opposite—A wall of sliding glass panels opens the kitchen to the house's waterfront deck. Fixed wooden louvers shade the windows above.
Below—The approach from the parking area threads between the garage and workshop, following a carefully framed view of the water.

very visibility that made the peninsula attractive in the first place. "The way the house looked from the water was very important to us. We wanted it to sit in the land. We didn't want it to be too obtrusive."

In that regard, architects Bruce Norelius and Matthew O'Malia found the site's post-industrial topography more an asset than an impediment. About the gravel pit they agreed, O'Malia says: "This is the ruined portion of the site; let's put the house here." From an entry courtyard that frames a water view between freestanding garage and workshop buildings, the house strings out along the shore in a series of connected pavilions that nestle into the south-facing bowl of the pit. Half-vaulted roof forms further minimize the building's profile while presenting a high wall of glass toward the south. The pavilions' long, narrow volumes allow south light to penetrate their full depth (aided in the bedroom wing by a continuous glass transom). Fixed wooden louvers control solar gain, while operable windows—low on the cool north side, high on

the south—promote natural ventilation. Zinc-coated copper roofs collect rainwater, which is filtered and stored in basement cisterns for domestic use.

When the weather is mild, the kitchen's south wall becomes an 8-foot-high, 20-foot-wide opening onto a waterfront deck. The master-bedroom wall performs a similar disappearing act. But the house reflects equal consideration of the northern winter. Meticulous weatherproofing deflects the pounding of Atlantic storms. Uncluttered interior spaces, simple geometry,

and clean, bright materials husband January's fleeting sunlight.

Every house starts with a hole in the ground, though, and before it was finished this one had generated a fair amount of controversy on the island. "It was so modern," says the owner. "And it was clad in blue Tyvek for two summers." The alarm, understandable at the time, has quieted now that the finished house has settled into the landscape. Its roofs hunch below the tree line, echoing the mounded shapes of the land; its

Top—Uncluttered spaces, light colors, and large windows stretch the daylight of Maine's northern winter. Above and left—A walnut cabinet hangs on the kitchen's bough-like steel columns.

Deer Isle House

dark-green clapboard walls, accented with mahogany doors and windows, blend into the coastal spruce backdrop. "One of the things that was important to us is that it not stand out as you approach the harbor," the owner says, "and in that we've been successful." She has scrutinized the scene closely enough to know. One night she and her husband lit all the lights, left the house, and rowed their dinghy out to see how it looked in the dark. Some of the fixtures in the bedroom wing looked too bright from the water, they concluded, "So we don't put them on much."

Right and below—The master bedroom and its deck nestle in a hollow in the landscape. Opposite—Very little stands between the owners of this house and the world outside.

Summer House

North Haven, Maine

Faced with the unlikely prospect of a sod-roofed Norwegian ski house on an island off the coast of Maine, one might guess that there was a good story behind it. One would be right. The original owners were an Eisenhower-era U.S. ambassador to Norway and his wife. Both fell in love with that country, but the ambassador's wife was especially smitten. On a trip to the mountains, she visited the family ski house of the charming young Norwegian woman who served as her companion and translator. She was so taken with the

building that she contacted its architect about designing something similar as a guest cottage for her own family's Maine summer home. The architect's son, who had taken over his father's firm, accepted the transatlantic commission. So, after a fashion, did the translator, who later met her charge's son and immigrated to the United States as his wife.

One of their daughters, who now shares ownership of the house, tells the story of its construction. "They wanted to make sure the house would go together properly," she says, "so they built it in Norway and weathered it for a year. They brought carpenters over from Norway and also employed quite a few people from the island, so it was a collaborative effort between Norwegians and islanders."

The building they produced has all the hallmarks of the traditional "hytte," or ski hut: log walls, a roof covered with sod dug from the site, and sleeping lofts accessible by ladders. "The layout is fairly contemporary, but the building methods were traditional for Norway. There's a lot of hand carving and folk art. The Norwegian winters are long and dark, so there's a lot of

Left—Inspired by traditional sod-roofed ski huts, this summer house transforms a Maine island meadow into an unlikely vision of Norway. Above—A miniature schoolhouse contains the sauna.

Below—Designed and fabricated in Norway, then assembled by Norwegian and American carpenters, the house shows its heritage in details born of long Nordic winters. The guest bedroom's sheltering built-in beds are among several sets in the house. Right--The living room's carved wooden columns and fireplace mantel are typical of traditional Norwegian log buildings.

craft work that gets done." The soapstone fireplace and wood mantel are ornately carved. The doors are decorated with colorful "rosemailing," folk-art painting that features abstract plant forms. The built-in beds, with their carved and painted wood surrounds, are straight out of a fairy tale. To her grandparents, the house was "a collection of all the things that represent Norway."

To their fifteen grandchildren, remembers this one,

it was less a cultural exhibit than simply a magical place to spend childhood summers. "One of the greatest things is that all you smell is wood when you walk into the house." Modeled on buildings designed for the long Norwegian winter, the hytte serves wonderfully as a summer place, too, she says, perhaps in part "because there are so many summer memories in the house." Some of her fondest are of rainy or foggy days,

In the structure itself, its furnishings, and the many mementos it holds, this house has served as a small, habitable piece of Norway for four generations of an American family.

"hunkering down from the elements. It felt like a wonderful place to tuck in and do puzzles, paint, play cards, make popcorn, have friends over. There are hiding places and nooks and crannies all over the house." It feels the same to her today, though now when the fog rolls in it is her own young daughter who conducts the explorations. And while there are no ski slopes or alpine meadows to explore when the weather clears, "It's so beautiful to step out the door and be right there on the ocean."

Burns/Spaulding House

Georgetown, Maine
Whitten Architects

If you were to come upon the house of Elizabeth Spaulding and Patrick Burns in Georgetown, Maine, say while scrambling the granite ledges that sprawl seaward from its porch or sailing the waters just beyond, chances are slim that you would take if for anything but an old house. Well tended, yes, recently spruced up perhaps, but not new. It has the comfortable look of a summer cottage built near the turn of the 20th century and added to or altered every decade or so since. Even those who knew the 1960s ranch-style house that recently occupied its very foundation will soon forget; the new house that grew in its place is that convincing.

Spaulding and Burns were living some distance inland when they first saw the site, which faces east

Opposite—A grandfathered location only steps from high water was the starting point for this year-round home. Above—Reclaimed windows offer wide open views of the Atlantic without upsetting the home's antique flavor.

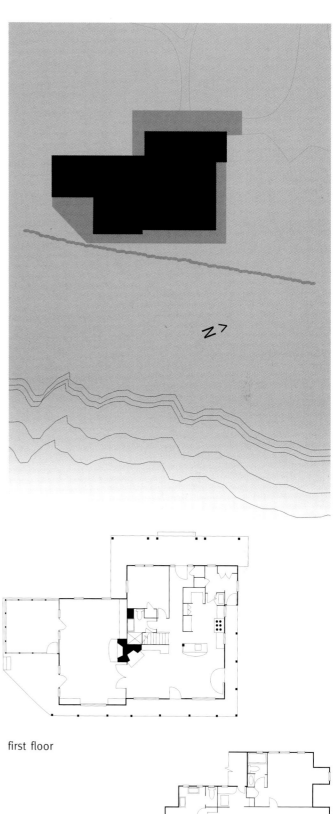

first floor

second floor

onto mid-coast Maine's Sheepscot Bay and south toward Seguin Island Lighthouse and the open Atlantic.

"We had to have it, of course," Burns says. And after more than fifteen years of calling this place home, he can say exactly why. "You get the full range of the sounds of the planet. You get the big winds, you get the big waves." Once a night owl, Burns says that the site's open easterly prospect soon had him rising with the sun, as early as 4:30 on summer mornings. "It put us in sync with the basic part of what living is all about," says Burns, who describes "the sense that you can see England on a clear day. It's almost worth getting into the kayak and seeing how far you can go." The constant presence of the sea "is profoundly engaging, and it really enriches our life here. Its range of moods matches ours, from tranquility to terror."

But while the owners relished living at this often stormy edge of the continent, their existing lightly built camp was overmatched by the elements. "The big easterly would blow in, and the whole house would shake," reports the couple's architect, Rob Whitten. Given their deep attachment to the site, his clients had strong opinions about its replacement. "They had been thinking about this for ten years," Whitten says, "and the last thing they wanted was something big, new, and out of scale." He could not have agreed more. A native son with a keen feel for Maine's vernacular architecture, Whitten worked upward from the existing building's footprint, applying an early-20th-century vocabulary of building shapes, proportions, details, and materials in a composition that is handsomely coherent but loose enough to

Right—The house's open easterly prospect has turned its owners into eager early risers. Below—A 10-year planning period gave the owners plenty of time to collect antique materials and furnishings. Opposite—An antique mantel, wearing its original paint, supplies instant age to the living room.

Right—Accessed by a pull-down attic stair, the third-floor bunk room is a secret paradise for the owners' grandchildren. The built-in berths add an appropriately nautical touch.

have evolved over decades rather than months.

Recently retired from a career as a business executive, Burns was free to oversee construction. With the new building's basic shell complete (the work of a general contractor), he took the helm, hammering out interior details with a pair of talented local woodworkers. "I had the great pleasure of being what I called the COW, the clerk of the works. I'd work on something late into the night," he says with a laugh, "and they'd come in the morning and very carefully take it apart." The design evolved as work proceeded. "We took a shipwright's approach to it," Burns says. "Every nook and cranny was to have a purpose." He and his wife contributed a trove of architectural antiques they had built

Above—In addition to period furniture, the owners collected antique pine boards to use as flooring. Right—The architect's intimate knowledge of Maine cottages, the builders' painstaking craftsmanship, and the owners' active engagement combined to produce a new house with an old soul.

up for the occasion, including two 18th-century mantels, a collection of old windows, and a generous stash of wide pine flooring boards. "The house therefore looks somewhat lived in all around," Burns says. The effect begins the moment the house comes into view, and it stands up under close inspection. And if the result is something of an illusion, neither dinner guests nor shoreline passersby will find it anything but grand.

Cameron Camp

Southport Island, Maine

Juan Cameron has known this place for almost eighty years, so he should know what to call it. "A camp, that's all it is," he says. Not a second home or a summer home or a cottage. A camp. For those who remember summer on the coast of Maine before air travel brought it so much closer to the rest of the country, the word evokes a very particular set of images: simple structures, lightly built, furnished with comfortable old stuff; family life transplanted, in those summers before air conditioning, to the cool of the north; fathers slipping away before dawn to catch the 5:00 a.m. train to the city for a week of work; children falling asleep to the sound of a june bug's buzzing against a window screen and the muffled laughter of adults out on the

porch. Memories of such things cling to a camp like the wood smoke Cameron and his wife, Nora, smell when they open the place up in the spring.

"I spent every summer of my life there," Cameron says, "from 1930 until today." His great-grandparents had bought the camp the year before, for $2,000. "It was very raw and primitive. The kitchen was on the back porch, and there was a three-seater outhouse. My family sank another $5,000 in it, to make a kitchen . . . and to get rid of the outhouse." Cameron's stories of those early summers are of childhood sailing adventures, a French governess "who hated it," and a life along the coast very different from what one sees here today. Lobstermen still set their traps just offshore, Cameron says, "But when I was a kid, it was twenty-five traps watched by rowboat. Now it's become five hundred to six hundred traps, and the rowboat has become a power lobster boat." Life onshore was different, too.

Right—Built in 1913, this summer camp has been in the owner's family since 1929. This living room addition dates from 1939. The schooner in the painting was one of 21 that the family once operated.

Opposite—The east-facing screened porch gathers the sun's warmth on cool summer mornings and provides shade during the heat of the day. Above and below—A 1980s renovation borrowed space from the kitchen for this water-view dining room.

"It being Prohibition, there was a flourishing gin-making operation in the garage and in the house."

Bathtub gin was history by the time Cameron brought his own children here for the summer, but he still rode the early Monday train to his newspaper job in Boston. And over the years, the camp has changed less than the world around it. A 1939 addition holds a living room downstairs and a master bedroom above. A deck extends from the "new" wing, perched on the ledges just above the high-tide mark. The Camerons remodeled again in the 1980s, removing partitions to create larger rooms and shifting the dining room from the back of the house to a position with an open view of the water.

Cameron Camp 79

But the building remains very much a camp. "It has no architectural pretensions," Cameron says. "It was built by fishermen or lobstermen in the winter." The cedar shingles come by their silver patina the old-fashioned way, by exposure to the weather. And the two stone fireplaces are not for show; with its open-stud walls, Cameron says, the building is "a thin strainer for the weather." Which is as it should be. "The season is governed by when the water is turned on, the 15th of April, and off, the 15th of October," he says. The rhythm of opening and closing the place each year sharpens the cycle of the seasons. The days between bring close the smell of the sea, the damp cool of the morning, the warmth of the fire. As it has always been for Cameron, so it is now for his grandchildren. This is what camp means.

Camps tend to accumulate old furniture and random artifacts, which over the years take on sentimental associations. Rarely, though, are such simple elements assembled with such a keen sense of color and composition.

Cavalli Beach House

Biddeford Pool, Maine

Myers & Yanko, architects

Even a day at the beach can present its challenges. The draw of the sandy shorefront being what it is, especially on the famously rock-bound coast of Maine, one must be ready to enjoy such places in the company of others. And one never knows who will lay out a blanket next door. But dedicated beach-goers find ways to adapt, accepting a certain degree of exposure in exchange for the pleasures of warm sand and salt water. And as it is for people, so it is for houses. Perched on its site like a sunbather on a blanket of sea grass, this weekend retreat in southern Maine nevertheless provides a surprisingly private experience of the shore.

It was the beach that drew owner Paul Cavalli to this spot, but with neighbors within Frisbee range, the

At Home by the Sea

feeling of solitude he sought would take some effort to realize. The nondescript story-and-a-half house that occupied the site fell far short of the mark. That building was disposed of relatively easily, but zoning rules required that any replacement fit within its modest,

nearly square footprint. "We couldn't even put a box-bay window in the dining room, because of the drip line," Cavalli says. Of particular concern, that limitation also seemed to rule out porches. "And I wanted porches."

Opposite — Only beach grass and sand stand between this house and the open Atlantic. Above left — Carefully placed windows dodge views of neighboring houses. Above right — Recessed porches open every major room to the outdoors.

first floor

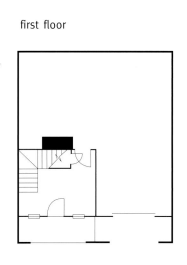

second floor

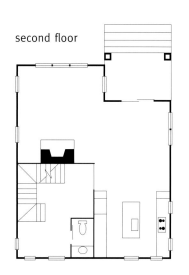

third floor

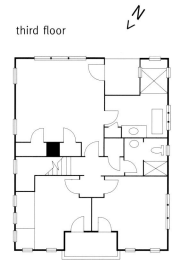

Above—High windows maximize the penetration of daylight into the building. Opposite—Every room enjoys a view of either ocean or salt marsh, even the master bathroom's walk-in shower.

The new house, penned by architect Lawrence Myers, squeezes two full stories of living space within the legal height limit. Inside, strategically placed windows frame views of the beach and a salt marsh at the house's inland side while dodging those of neighboring houses. Two windowless stretches of wall provide backdrops for a relaxed interior stair and a large painting entitled, fittingly, The Beach. Myers solved the porch conundrum by carving outdoor rooms from the building's basic volume, rather than hanging them outside of it. The first floor's large corner porch, whose full-width stair descends to the beach grass, "has become the primary living area,"

Myers reports. The master bedroom opens onto a small, private porch just above, while the two guest bedrooms share a third, which offers views of the salt marsh but privacy from the immediate neighbors.

The need to maximize living space within the legal height limit dictated a tall, narrow form topped with a shallow-pitched roof, a potentially ungainly combination. But Myers made a virtue of necessity, wrapping the building in a loosely interpreted Greek Revival style that leavens the austerity of a 19th century saltwater farmhouse with a touch of boardwalk theatricality. The result, Cavalli says, works like a charm. "Even though it's only 2,000 square feet, it feels spacious and

Opposite—A painting entitled "The Beach" occupies a place designed specifically for it. This page—An efficient kitchen and bright, crisp interior detailing make this house as welcoming in winter as it is in summer.

At Home by the Sea

Standing on a narrow lot in a densely developed strip of shore-front, this weekend house pulls off the deft trick of screening out its neighbors while making the beach its own.

comfortable." Large windows with minimal coverings and transom lights that reach almost to the ceiling, light colors, and minimalist detailing keep the interior bright on cloudy days. Those qualities—plus proper year-round construction—mean that there is no off season at this beach. "The wintertime is almost nicer," Cavalli says. "There's nothing like going up there on a Saturday and lighting a fire, and keeping the fire going until Sunday evening when we leave."

Cavalli Beach House 91

Nolen/Denny Vacation House

Cape Cod, Massachusetts

Breese Architects

"When I started going to the Cape, there was no mall," Christian Nolen says. "There was one pizzeria you could eat at. The day after Labor Day the Cape was abandoned." Nolen, age 46, spent his childhood summers near Hyannis, on Great Island, a substantial part of which had been in his family for generations. "The houses that were out there," he remembers, "none of them were fancy. None of them were heated. Their foundations were a cinderblock turned on its side." Today, after an explosion of growth in tourism, year-round population, and prestige, Cape Cod is a very different place. But here on Great Island, things don't feel that different at all, largely due to the way in which Nolen's family developed its land. "There are conservation easements on most of it," he says. "There are forty houses in a square mile. In relation to most of Cape Cod it's really quiet." When an adjacent property became available, Nolen and his wife, Susan

Opposite—A simple boardwalk connects this low-profile vacation home with the nearby beach. Above—The screened porch serves as an outdoor dining room.

Denny, did not hesitate to buy it, even though, as he says, "this one came with some interesting restrictions."

Consisting largely of dunes and wetlands and lying in a flood zone, the site was both too fragile and too exposed for a conventional building, but it was a precious remnant of what Nolen calls "raw Cape Cod." In planning a year-round vacation house here, he and Denny intended to disturb that condition as little as possible. "You see enough houses on the Cape," Nolen says. "We just wanted to disappear." The house that architect Peter Breese designed for the couple and their two children lands admirably close to that target. The building's timber-piling foundation required neither concrete nor excavation. Its form—narrow, single-story wings crossing in a drawn-out X—minimizes its visual impact on the nearby beach. Despite the fact that it perches ten feet off the ground (safe from a storm surge), "When you're out on the ocean, this house is basically invisible," Nolen says. "You have to look for it to see it."

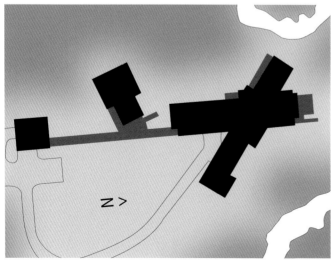

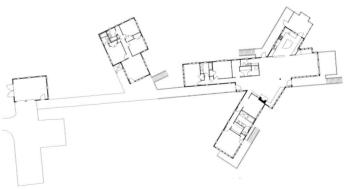

A foundation of driven wood pilings minimizes disturbance to the fragile site and raises the building above a potential storm tide. It also affords tree-top access to light and views.

Nolen/Denny Vacation House

Visibility from inside, though, is an entirely different matter. The building's long wings present a deceptively broad surface area toward Hyannis Harbor. "It's all about what you see outside," Nolen says. "If you stand in the living room you have a 180-degree water view." He and his wife call the place "Ferryland," for the Nantucket boats that pass throughout the day. "We are the closest house to the channel," Nolen says. "It's an amazing ringside seat." The building's leggy floor plan brings other benefits as well: openness and an appealing complexity at the kitchen/dining/living area, which occupies the intersection of the X; one-room-deep wings for plentiful daylight and natural ventilation; privacy for the bedroom suites; and, in spite of the building's ample size, a cottage-scale roof over every room.

This page—The open kitchen encourages a participatory approach to communal meals and a free flow between cooking and dining areas. Opposite—Long, narrow wings give most rooms windows on at least two walls.

Left—An X-shaped floor plan yields views that telescope through the house toward Hyannis Harbor. Top—Simple exterior detailing reflects the harsh conditions the building will sometimes face on this ocean-exposed site. Above—The entry walk floats above sand and marsh grass.

Breese filled out the plan's basic form with bay windows, covered porches, and a long boardwalk that ties the main house to a separate guest cottage and the parking area. The latter is deliberately distant and well hidden, the better to quell unwelcome thoughts of leaving.

Harper's Island House

Chatham, Massachusetts
Polhemus Savery DaSilva Architects Builders

It is said that hard cases make bad law. In architecture, though, it is often the hardest cases that elicit the most inspired solutions. Witness this vacation home, which sits on its own 1.5-acre island in a salt pond at the edge of Nantucket Sound. Accessible only by a one-hundred-yard-long footbridge, the island was home to two small, dilapidated cottages dating from the 1940s. Those two buildings would make way for this new one, but their spectral shapes would linger in the form of regulatory constraints. The new building would have to stand within the footprints of the old ones (plus a small piece connecting the two) and rise no higher than their twelve- and thirteen-foot roofs. The narrow bridge forced the builders to carry all their tools and materials to the island by hand or in motorized wheelbarrows. The island's fragile environment

Occupying its own island, with no neighboring structures as context, this vacation house takes its design cues from the immediate natural environment. The brackets that support its broadly overhanging eaves mimic the forms of tree branches.

presented still more challenges. But no matter; this is the kind of briar patch some architects live for. And the design/build firm of Polhemus Savery DaSilva responded with a house that owes its unique character as much to the limitations placed on it as to the special qualities of its site.

Project architect John DaSilva began by allocating the footprint of the larger cottage to common spaces and a pair of guest rooms. The smaller cottage's square footage went to a new master bedroom. To maximize interior volume, he gave the former a flat roof twelve

Opposite—While its sequence of forms and spaces unfolds naturally, the building's footprint was predetermined by those of two old cottages that once stood here. Above—Views that extend through adjacent rooms and into the landscape make the modestly scaled entry seem larger than it is.

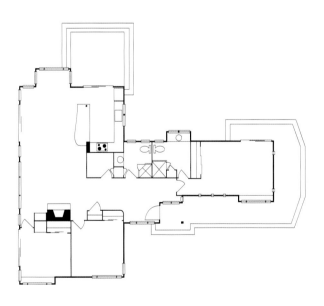

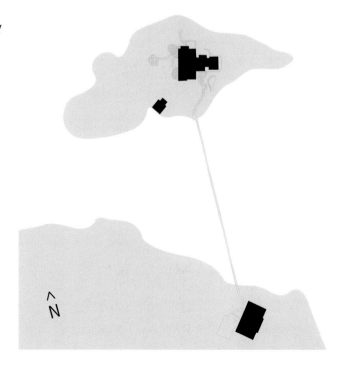

feet high and the latter a shallow vaulted roof that slips in under the thirteen-foot limit. A lower flat roof with a pyramidal skylight tops the entry. The main roofs spread into long overhangs, extending their shelter beyond the outside walls and strengthening the building's visual presence. Angled brackets support the eaves, their form borrowed from the island's wind-shaped trees. Gently arched window mullions pick up the arboreal theme.

Inside, DaSilva employed some subtle touches to make the building's 1,600 square feet feel and function like a lot more. A low ceiling over the entry emphasizes the height of the main ceilings. A band of high transom windows that rings the house reinforces the effect. Built-in furniture and cleverly concealed storage make efficient use of the limited floor space. Fine-tuned sightlines run along the building's axes and out into the landscape. With its wall of windows facing west toward

Opposite—A band of high clerestory windows emphasizes the living room's height and opens the room to the sky. Above—A lower ceiling and suspended display shelves help delineate the kitchen.

the pond, the living and dining area enjoys the semi-enclosed feeling of a front porch. The tiny windows that pierce the master-bedroom walls not only satisfy the need for both daylight and privacy from the adjacent

Opposite—Inventive window design plays on our expectations of shape, scale, and placement. Above—A patio and low stone wall define a casual outdoor dining area, one of several informal living spaces that extend into the landscape.

decks, but also create an optical illusion, their unexpected size making them seem farther away than they are.

The house's location works a similar trick. That narrow bridge, only 300 feet long, crosses to another world. And in spite of the extraordinary measures required in approval, design, and construction, the house seems very much at home here, its faintly exotic form removing the island even farther from that other, ordinary world. Its owners liken it to a jewel box in the middle of a nature preserve and claim that the mere sight of it across the salt marsh has a calming effect. Sometimes, in exchange for the privilege of occupying an extraordinary spot on the earth, a house must jump through more than its share of hoops, and this one has. But you would never know by looking at it.

Opposite above—A one-hundred-yard-long footbridge is the only means of access to this private island.

Roach House

Nantucket, Massachusetts
McMillen Interior Design and Decoration

George and Maria Roach's first visit to Nantucket, thirty-five years ago, marked the beginning of two enduring relationships. "We were newlyweds," says George Roach. "We went up on Labor Day weekend, and it rained the whole weekend. And we fell in love with it." Given the weather, one might assume that Nantucket did not win their hearts with its beaches,

fine as they are. The key from the start, and for every summer since, has been the island's unmatched collection of preserved 18th- and 19th-century architecture. "It was the historic homes," says George Roach. "It was the homes that never died."

It is fitting, then, that the house the Roaches eventually bought and restored is itself a repository of

Above--When whaling captain Seth Pinkham built this house in the early 19th century, its widow's walk looked out on one of the busiest ports in the world. Opposite—The restored façade opens onto a street scene that Pinkham himself might still find familiar.

Nantucket history. Built in the early 19th century by whaling captain Seth Pinkham, the house reflects both the island's austere Quaker heritage and the riches it earned in the whaling trade, then at its height. The two-and-a-half-story main house fronts directly on a brick sidewalk near the center of town, its weathered shingle walls and scant overhangs reflecting the Quaker period's no-nonsense attitude toward shelter. A classically framed front door and transom hint at the more elaborate workmanship within, though, where molded trim dresses up walls, windows, doors, and stairs. An original cast-iron fireplace insert, still in service, speaks of the social standing of its original owner. "This was, at the time, to show that you could afford to go to France," Roach says, "and that you could afford to bring this home."

And while the whaling trade built this house, the passing of that enterprise may have been instrumental in preserving it. During the decades of economic eclipse that followed the transition from whale oil to petroleum, there was simply not enough money on the island to update or replace such old buildings. By the time prosperity returned, in the pockets of 20th-century tourists, the old buildings had become treasured relics. As a result, when the Roaches bought this house most of its period features—and such original details as wrought iron door hardware—were intact. Which left

Above—The owners insisted on an accurate restoration of the original house's plaster, woodwork, and door hardware. Opposite—In reworking an earlier modern addition, they opted for a looser interpretation of traditional Nantucket style.

the still-formidable task of restoration. With the help of architect Ed Jenkins and interior designer Mary Louise Guertler, the Roaches turned back the clock, restoring plaster, reproducing missing trim moldings and hardware, and applying paint colors that subtly highlight the house's antique craftsmanship.

"It's a quirky house," says Jenkins, "in that you have to go through rooms to get to other rooms, which is typical of the period." But the restoration respected the original layout of the main house. The Roaches took a freer approach with the attached carriage barn to the rear, converting what was a single, open space into a family room/guest suite with a sleeping loft

Above—Amateur historians, the owners furnished the house largely with goods from the 19th century. Right—Originally the birthing room, this small den houses a collection of antique English Toby mugs and framed souvenir flags from Japan.

Left—Indian baskets and framed displays of silk cigar ribbons line the front stair. Opposite—At the rear of the house, a sleeping loft serves as guest quarters for visiting grandchildren.

above. "You start out in the house in the 19th century," Jenkins says, "and as you move toward the back, you end up in the 21st."

What the Roaches like best about this house, though, is its ability to run that process in reverse. Stepping out the front door takes them to a time when people did their in-town business on foot, encountering neighbors along the way. The wooden walk that crowns their roof looks down on a harbor that was, two hundred years ago, the busiest whaling port in the world. And in the front room hangs a portrait of Captain Seth Pinkham. In 1821, off the coast of Chile, his ship, the *Dauphin*, rescued the captain and another surviving crewman of the whaling ship *Essex*, whose sinking by a whale inspired Melville's *Moby Dick*. "Every time I go in there I say 'hello,'" Roach says. "I say, 'Hey, I'm keeping your house.'"

Jeffers House

Martha's Vineyard, Massachusetts
Polshek Partnership Architects

Wendy Jeffers is a painter and curator, so it was only natural that she and her husband, Anthony Orphanos, approach the design of their Martha's Vineyard vacation home less as architectural clients than as patrons of the arts. Their choice of the Manhattan architecture firm Polshek Partners was a creative act in itself. "I was familiar with Polshek's work in museums," says Jeffers. But as firm partner and proj-

ect architect Richard Olcott notes, "What we do is institutional and cultural buildings and schools. We don't do houses." Good architects relish a good problem, though, and Olcott found this one too intriguing to refuse: "They wanted the outside to look like it had been there for three hundred years and the inside to be totally modern."

The site, five acres of tree-dotted meadow with

views of Squibnocket Pond and open ocean, offered an inviting canvas. It also presented challenges that shaped the project's ultimate form. "It's a very visible site, for the island," Jeffers says. "We felt there was an enormous responsibility to do something that blended in with the landscape, that didn't impose itself." To determine what that might be, Olcott conducted an informal field study of the local architecture. At the first design presenta-

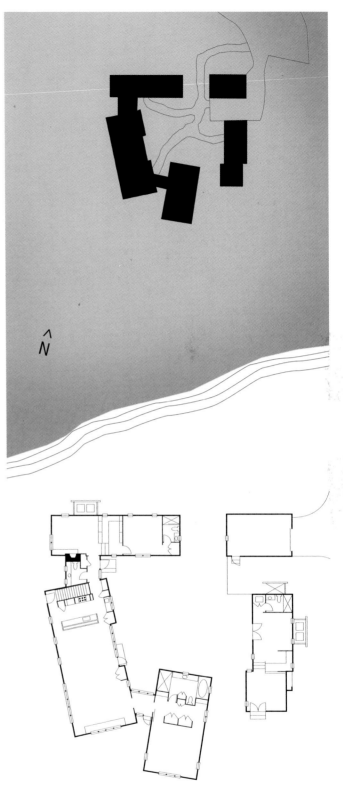

tion, Jeffers remembers, "They had taken one of their large conference rooms and covered it with pictures of barns." She and her husband were thrilled.

Olcott's plan consists of five pavilions with the aus-

Rather than dominate its very open, visible site with a massive structure, this home spreads its square footage among five single-story pavilions. The compound's spare, shingle-clad shapes recall traditional island farm buildings.

Jeffers House 121

tere forms and gray shingle surfaces of weathered barns. "To break its scale down, we built five small buildings instead of one big one," Olcott says. The scheme created the means to engage other features of the site as well. "There is this constant ten- or fifteen-knot breeze off the ocean," Olcott says, "which is gently sandblasting everything." His pavilions surround a grassy courtyard, creating a protected outdoor space and directing views both between and through the structures. "We spent an incredible amount of time staking it out," Olcott says,

"rotating all the pieces to get that to work just the right way, so you could see the ocean and the pond and the sun going down over the pond."

Having willingly surrendered its exterior forms to the island's aesthetic gestalt, the building advances a very different agenda inside. The owners have lived in a SoHo loft for the past thirty years, Olcott, observes. "They're into that whole idea of openness." This vacation home, therefore, is "free-plan, open, and loft-like inside, very sparely detailed, very flush, as simple as it

Top left—A semi-enclosed central courtyard provides shelter from the constant sea breeze. Top right and above—The loft-like interior draws on a limited palette of materials, spare detailing, and simple geometry to generate an atmosphere that is both serene and refreshing.

Jeffers House   123

Above—Like the living pavilion, the master bedroom reflects a bias toward symmetry, aligning its major elements on an axis defined by the ridge of the roof above. Opposite—The stair to the living pavilion's lower level establishes a secondary axis perpendicular to the ridge.

could be, really." The rooms are large and uncluttered. The material palette is minimal: beech floors and cabinets, white-painted wood ceilings, Brazilian blue-granite counters, "and not much else."

Jeffers and Orphanos are delighted with the outcome, but Jeffers speaks with equal enthusiasm about the process that led to it. Olcott and his firm "don't do houses," but that seems to have worked in their favor. "Because they don't do houses, everything was new. It

became a pet project for them." And with all of the firm's industrial-strength skill and professionalism focused on this comparatively miniature project, creative sparks were bound to fly. "They have terrific communication skills," Jeffers says, "and I think because of their ability to ask questions we got some really great answers." Questions and answers, images and responses, rolls of trace paper covered in sketches—"We were just enchanted. We were part of it. It was as exciting as it gets."

With its textured, weathered, agrarian-inspired shell and polished, cosmopolitan interior, this house reveals something of the character of its owners, Manhattanites with deep ties to Martha's Vineyard.

Two Cottages

Martha's Vineyard, Massachusetts

Hutker Architects

It has been said that the inside of a house belongs to its owners, but the outside belongs, in part, to the neighbors. That is especially true when the house is the backdrop for a pristine and cherished beach, a fact that made the renovation of these two Martha's Vineyard summer cottages a rather delicate matter.

"Development is kind of a dirty word on Martha's Vineyard," says architect Phil Regan. The zoning regulations here are stringent, the authorities skeptical, and the neighbors fiercely protective of their island's natu-

The Kane cottage began life as a simple fishing camp. An extensive remodel fitted it out for year-round use without entirely obscuring those roots.

ral environment and cultural legacy. But Regan threaded the needle with these two extensive rebuilds, which occurred nearly simultaneously and within sight of each other, satisfying the "owners" outside as well as those inside.

The buildings, which stand watch on Vineyard Sound to the north, began life as modest, seasonal structures, and neither strays far from that heritage. Both are compact, with bleached wood-shingle walls and low roofs that look drifted up, like the surrounding dunes. Traditional details such as divided-light double-hung

first floor

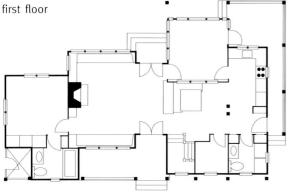

second floor

Opposite—The relatively narrow, window-lined living room wing allows daylight to pour through. Above—A fragile site and protective neighbors made planning and approval of this house a delicate matter.

Two Cottages/Kane 131

windows and exposed rafter tails reinforce the camp connection and give these neighbors a clear family resemblance.

Katherine Kane and Olin West had summered on the island for ten years when they bought their cottage. "We decided, not very seriously, to look for what was available," Kane says, "and we found what was called a fishing camp on the far north shore, in the remotest town on the island. It's just a beautiful spot, and at that time it was affordable." Along with their two sons, they took possession in the spring, journeying north from their home in Charlottesville, Virginia, somewhat ahead of the warm weather. "We set up space heaters in

this un-insulated, crate-wood cottage," Kane remembers. The remodel that soon followed made the building comfortable in all four seasons without confusing the fact that this remains a vacation home. Open ceilings show the bones of the cottage. Pale painted surfaces make the most of the available natural light, while a boat-like efficiency of planning makes the fullest use of the limited interior volume. Built-in seating anchors the dining area and lines the window walls of the living room. A day bed turns the tiny, sunny upstairs hall into a reading nook and overflow guest space. "I wanted the interior to match the serenity out the window," says Kane, who drew inspiration from the brightness and

Opposite—A built-in day bed turns this small hallway into a reading nook and guest bedroom. Above—Banquettes that line two walls of the living room add space-efficient seating.

calm of traditional Swedish homes. A poet and novelist, she loves her family vacations here, but says the cottage's highest calling is as a writer's retreat. "It's so peaceful."

Mollie and John Callagy share the neighboring cottage—and a somewhat more active scenario—with John's brother and his family. "We flip back and forth months during the summer," says Callagy of their time-sharing arrangement. "The house is occupied pretty fully from June 15th to October 1st." After more than a decade of hard use, the house was due for a remodel, and rather than spoil the stew with too many cooks, the Callagys turned the project over to their architect. "I have to say it was totally and completely driven by the site, and by Phil and what he could do with the site," Callagy says. With families of four and five in tag-team residence, square footage is even more precious than at Kane and West's house, next door. Regan organized the

building in an elegant bunkhouse/mess-hall arrangement, wrapping private spaces for sleeping and bathing around a larger room that accommodates all other indoor activities. Capped with an open-rafter hipped roof, the kitchen/living/dining room turns its high-win-dowed outside walls toward a generous deck, an undulating field of beach grass, the dunes, and blue water.

The house represents a deceptively sophisticated piece of work, combining historical depth and local character with Modernist space planning, but in func-

Above—Here, everything occurs against the backdrop of the sky descending to meet the sea. Opposite—The low, open-rafter roof over this bedroom recalls the building's rustic beginnings.

Opposite—Serving families of four and five—alternately—the Callagy cottage makes elegantly efficient use of its limited square footage. A bunkhouse/mess hall floor plan concentrates daytime functions in a single open common room that faces the beach. Above—Its two seaward walls lined to the roof with windows, the kitchen/living/dining room uses the outward view to expand its perceived volume.

tion it is the soul of simplicity. "We both have pretty complicated houses at home," says Callagy, who appreciates the contrast of this family retreat. "It's simple to open up, and it's simple to close down. You walk in, you

Left—A simple square plan and an open-rafter hip roof above tie the common room together as a single space, while furniture delineates separate seating and function areas.

open the windows, and that's pretty much it." Much of the family's attention is focused outdoors anyway, he reports. "We have a small outboard. We play golf. We fish. We ride bikes. We enjoy the sunsets, which are second to none in that location. People have told me it's the only place on the East Coast where the sun sets over water." And when the family retreats indoors, the intimate scale of the building heightens their sense of distance from everyday life. "It forces everything to be kind of pared down. We have no TV. It's a place for different activities. You take a break from what you ordinarily do."

Above—From its open deck, the building seems to sail on an ocean of wild grass. Its location, on the island's western shore, affords the rare sight of a Massachusetts sunset over the ocean. Opposite— Light-colored surfaces and large banks of windows combine to make the interior nearly as bright as the outdoors. The slanting afternoon light adds tints of red and gold.

Writer's Cottage

Martha's Vineyard, Massachusetts

South Mountain Company

South Mountain Company, Martha's Vineyard's masters of green building, hatched this little gem as part of an annual affordable-housing fundraiser. "What we set out to do," says company president John Abrams, "was to make the most highly crafted building we could out of found stuff." And a colorful bunch of stuff they found: gnarled framing timbers from the island's native white oaks; lumber from a dismantled dairy barn in Vermont; forty-year-old wooden wall shingles from a house the company renovated; window frames of redwood salvaged from a brewery's beer tanks; door handles and coat hooks of native blueberry branches. The centerpiece, a built-in desk, is a single plank of cypress sawn from an aged log that was

Opposite—The wind-shaped trunks of island oaks frame this tiny structure, which the owner uses as a summer office. Above—Stained glass fills the crooks of the corner posts.

dredged from a river bottom in Georgia. The builders got friends to donate other charming bits and pieces, roofed the shack with discarded aluminum printing plates from the *Vineyard Gazette* (placing an old story about the island's affordable-housing crisis in plain view), and put it on the auction block.

"We saw this cranky little shack, and I just fell in love with it," says the woman who bought it, an actress and filmmaker who summers on the island's south end. She directed the builders to set the shack down near her garden, where she can easily admire it. "It's my favorite spot on the property," she says. "It looks like there's not a straight line in it, but it's actually beauti-

fully crafted. All the joints and joists and bits . . . It looks like it grew there overnight, or after a nor'easter blew in and deposited it there." And while it makes a fine lawn ornament, the building also serves as her working office through the summer months. "It's got a little solar panel, so I can run a computer in there," she points out. "It's got all the mod cons, but in a really ecological way." With its desktop window facing east toward the sea and the rising sun, the building is warm on chilly mornings, shady in the heat of the day, redolent of wood, and filled with gentle diversions. "If you're bored or need inspiration, you just lie on the floor and look up and read."

Above left—The windows reuse redwood from discarded brewery tanks. Above right—The walls wear 40-year-old salvaged shingles. Opposite—Old aluminum printing plates, legible from below, cover the roof.

Vacation House

Rhode Island
Shope Reno Wharton Architecture

The owners of this new vacation home on the Rhode Island shore had plenty of decisions to make during the course of its design and construction, but the matter of architectural style was never in question. Their property, nineteen acres of shorefront land on a causeway-access island, settled the matter for them, says architect Bernard Wharton. "They wanted to do a house that was in keeping with the island's architecture, which meant Shingle Style." They came to the right man. One of the style's foremost contemporary practitioners, Wharton also knew the island well. "I had been going to that place my whole life," he says. This stretch of the New England coast was the birthplace of the Shingle Style, and the shoreline here is

Opposite—Built a century after the Shingle Style first appeared, this summer home demonstrates the enduring appeal of the this uniquely American coastal architecture. Above—Shaded by a pergola, the second-floor deck surveys 19 acres of shorefront property.

studded with the surviving works of its founding luminaries, Henry Hobson Richardson and McKim, Mead & White. Commissioned more than one hundred years ago by members of a Gilded Age upper class then pioneering the concept of summers at the shore, these sprawling "summer cottages" look as sound today as the day they were built. And as this new house demonstrates, the Shingle Style itself is thriving, too.

"At the turn of the century, people were looking for a style that was not so formal," Wharton says, "somewhat rusticated, but with a great sense of fun and whimsy about it." The same was true of Wharton's clients, a Philadelphia couple with two grown chil-

dren, who gather here several times a year. They chose the location for its dramatic shoreline—a wall of rocky cliffs—and their house reflects that focus. Five pairs of French doors open the building's central dining room and great room onto a broad stone terrace to seaward. Large covered porches and a second-floor deck offer more sheltered vantage points. The floor plans of the original cottages were rather open for their day, and Wharton advanced that theme even further here, using traditionally trimmed openings to delineate living spaces rather than walls to divide them. But while the old Shingle cottages were designed for summer use, this one is fitted out for year-round living. "The

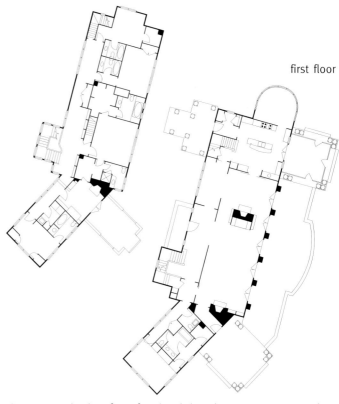

second floor

first floor

Opposite—The shorefront façade exhibits the impressive size and balanced asymmetry characteristic of the Shingle Style. Left—A stained floor pattern breaks down the scale of the long entry hall.

Below—Unlike the great 19th-century "cottages" it emulates, this home has a kitchen fit for company. Below left and opposite—Traditional detailing clothes a rather contemporary open floor plan.

detailing is such that you would be comfortable here on a cold winter day in a driving snow," Wharton says. "It has these cozy, intimate spaces, and it has spaces more geared to entertaining and outdoor life. I think the beauty of the house is, it can do both. The plan is

actually quite modern, with a traditional skin."

In spite of the quaint moniker, the original cottages were impressively large, and this one runs true to form. But the style's extensive vocabulary of human-scale elements yields a house that carries its size gracefully. The

roof cascades from its high ridge to an eave line that rings the building at first-story level. Dormers of varied shapes and sizes perch on its slopes. Windows cluster in framed groupings under pediments and shingled eyebrows. There is plenty here to keep the eye busy, but it

Above—Small panes and transom lights give this master bedroom window a period feeling without slighting the view outside. Opposite—the adjoining bath offers a similar view, with an added measure of enclosure.

Above—Strong horizontal elements balance the building's significant height. Opposite—Occupying a high-profile site near the birthplace of the Shingle Style, this latter day example looks as much at home as any of its stylistic forebears.

is more than mere visual noise. The rambling asymmetry of the composition grows out of symmetrical parts—the main building, the garage/guest wing, porches, dormers, window assemblies—each of which embodies its own internal logic. Strong horizontal bands of dark painted trim ground the verticality of the

high gables, the projecting stair tower, and two tapering stone chimneys. A restrained surface of cedar shingles wraps a coherent package that looks perfectly at home in both its setting and in its day. This, say the owners, is the house their site was looking for. "We really wanted something that would be timeless, and we got that."

McKenna House

Hilton Head, South Carolina

Group 3 Architects

The vacationers who flock to Hilton Head, South Carolina, each year know a good thing when they see it. The climate here is delightful most of the time, the beaches broad and smooth, the natural environment and outdoor sports outstanding. Those who have made this barrier island their year-round home, though, are really onto something. Ask Deedy and John McKenna, who moved here from Atlanta ten years ago. They both have their hands full, working

and raising two young sons. But doing it here, within steps of the Atlantic, allows them to weave a thread of vacation-like experiences into the fabric of their daily lives. "We plan our weekends based on the weather report," says Deedy McKenna. "We wake up in the morning and look at the wind. Do you sail or do you golf? It all depends on the weather and the tide." And the primary vehicle for this best-of-both-worlds arrangement is the house they built, a year-round

home that functions like a single-family resort.

Occupying nearly the full width of its beachfront lot, the house presents a reserved facade to the street, with twin garages at ground level and a small, gated courtyard guarding the entrance. Inside the front door, though, the house springs to life. Tall glazed doors and windows with high transoms light the interior. The entry hall sites down an axis that runs through the building, across the pool, lawn, and beach, and straight on to the horizon. The primary living space is the "beach room," which spreads across the rear of the

house, opening onto a covered veranda. "One flexible room, two seating groups," says Architect Mike Ruegamer, echoing his clients' request. Ruegamer designed the room's furniture arrangement and circulation paths to channel site lines through its three sets of French doors. That move, he says, "kind of dictated the rest of the layout," which works back toward the street with a kitchen and dining room aligned with the beach room's openings. In a variation on stadium seating, a three-step rise in floor level improves the beach views from these second-row spaces. The second-floor plan

first floor

second floor

follows a similar scheme. The master bedroom, flanked by twin terraces and a pair of dressing room/offices, occupies the beach side of the house. The children's bedrooms and guest rooms march in orderly fashion toward the street.

In the character of the house, McKenna says, "We wanted to blend in the architecture from the West Indies, from Charleston, and—believe it or not—a little bit of the northeast." The building's hipped roofs are clad in clay tiles. The exposed rafter tails bear a decorative sawn profile. Exterior walls combine board-

Above left—A full-width covered veranda opens the oceanfront façade of this year-round home. The twin balconies above are a step down from the second floor level, so their railings do not obscure the view from within. Above—A gated courtyard guards the approach from the street.

Above—Rough tabby stucco walls sound a casual note in a house whose planning and details are otherwise quite formal. Opposite—The second-floor master bedroom enjoys an unobstructed view to the Atlantic horizon.

and-batten siding and "tabby," a traditional, regional concrete formula that incorporates crushed oyster shells. "We wanted it to have some age, and to blend into the trees," McKenna says. "I kept saying to the architects, 'I want the tabby to be the color of the sand, when it's wet.'" Exposed at the interior of the beach-front rooms, the material introduces a rough earthiness that contrasts with the building's formal symmetry and details. Louvered interior doors, dark-stained pine roof timbers, and woven sea-grass mats on the floors further the theme of casual living in a refined setting. Taken together, it adds up to the perfect formula for a small inn or bed & breakfast by the shore. But for a year-round house? Now you're talking.

This page—The architecture interweaves design themes from the British West Indies, Charleston, and even New England. Opposite— This house's location and amenities make it a virtual single-family resort.

Caribbean Vacation House

St. Barthelemy
BSSW Architects

Basking in the perpetual summer of the French West Indies, the shores of St. Barthelemy encompass some of the most sought-after real estate on earth. But blue water and balmy weather notwithstanding, that exclusivity derives in part from the fact that there is simply so little of St. Barth to go around. Eight-and-a-half square miles in extent, the island's mountainous terrain yields small, steep building sites, and precious few of those. Some five centuries after Europeans first laid eyes on this pint-sized paradise, says architect Chuck Schmitt, "There's very little land left for development. And there's been a very big movement to keep the mountainsides green." This house, for which Schmitt designed an extensive remodel, is unusual.

Opposite—The weather on St. Barth is nearly perfect, except when a hurricane blows, so the common room of this home offers as little or as much shelter as necessary. *Above left*—The ajoupa stands in a pool of water lilies. *Below left*—From the terrace, one can see as far as St. Maarten.

Despite "a rather smashing view," he says, "it is not clinging to the mountainside." But while large, level, elevated sites are rare here, the original house took less than full advantage of this one. Its back garden was paved in concrete, Schmitt reports. "It had one tree." Retained by a U.S. client to put things in order, Schmitt responded with a design that weaves seaward, landward, and interior spaces into a single, expansive living environment.

The building's flying-V floor plan, a legacy of its original design, points like an arrow toward St. Jean Beach, far below. The form was clearly chosen to maximize water views, but Schmitt developed its inland side as well, extending the west wing with a new master-bedroom pavilion and the east wing with a covered gatehouse that joins the house to its garden wall. Thus enclosed, the fully landscaped garden centers on an "ajoupa," or garden pavilion, which rises from a pool floating with water lilies. An overflowing ceramic urn fills the pool via a narrow channel that marks a watery axis from the ajoupa through the house and on to the horizon.

To achieve a degree of openness appropriate to the climate, Schmitt says, "We tore down roughly 35 or 40 percent of the home." And, indeed, the resulting building provides the requisite measure of shelter while disappearing as much as possible. "We made a conscious effort to erase that image of the perimeter wall," he says. "The house is wide open. Birds fly through; birds sit on lampshades." Designed to serve an extended family that reunites here on holiday, the house spreads out in a series of connected pavilions. "It appears as a home that has grown through the years, which is fairly common on the island," Schmitt says. Each of the four bedrooms acts as a semi-independent suite, with its own bath, deck, and outdoor shower. Circulation between rooms occurs largely outdoors.

Caribbean Vacation House   169

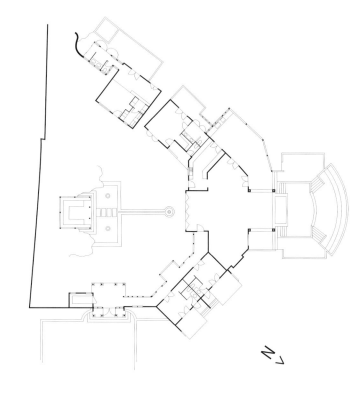

Opposite above—A covered terrace with its own kitchen suits an extended family that enjoys preparing outdoor communal meals. Opposite below—Like the house's other bathing facilities, the master bathroom includes an outdoor shower.

Group activities cluster at the center of the house, where a generous great room opens onto a deep covered porch. "It's a sort of family tradition to gather and cook outdoors," says Schmitt, who equipped the porch with an open-air kitchen and room enough for the entire clan to share a single table. The great room's terra cotta floor

Below—The master bedroom steps down to clear sight lines toward the water. Right—This outdoor shower serves one of the secondary bedrooms. Below right—Each bedroom functions as a semi-independent suite, with its own private deck. Opposite—Two levels of outdoor pool and several levels of terrace step down from the level of the common room, leaving open views to the shore, nearby islands, and the horizon.

disappears into the surface of a wading pool, which spills into a larger swimming pool below. To preserve water views, the outdoor living spaces step downhill from the house, from the porch to the pool deck to a fan-shaped terrace, from which the island, in turn, falls away in a green apron toward the sea. On a clear day you can see St. Maarten in the distance, or watch small inbound planes clear a saddle in the mountains by mere feet. And toast them for having brought you here.

Roosevelt House

Named for Christopher Columbus's brother, its only major town built by Swedes, and with a population that is mostly French, the Caribbean Island of St. Barthelemy is the product of many cultures. The same can be said of this house. Built in the 1980s by German architect Miles Reinke, it goes by the name Maison Mexicaine. Reinke recruited Mexican workers, explains owner Laura Roosevelt, "And they really built it in the style of a Mexican hacienda." Roosevelt first laid eyes on the house in the mid-1990s, when she rented it from a certain Russian-born ballet superstar. "The house has just been full of artists and dancers and musicians," she says. "I often say, 'If these walls could talk...'" Roosevelt and her partner, Russ Gerson, bought the house soon after and embarked on a major remodel that drew on the talents of tradespeople from across the Western Hemisphere. "We had all these workers there speaking this multitude of languages," Roosevelt

Opposite—Perched above St. Jean Bay, this island retreat enjoys views of volcanic peaks and blue water. Above—The building's design owes as much to the classic Mexican hacienda as it does to local Caribbean architecture.

says. "Portuguese, French, English, German, Spanish ..." For all this, though, the building carries its history lightly. Architecturally, Roosevelt says, "It doesn't relate to anything on the island. It is unique." But like St. Barth's many sophisticated expatriates, Mais Mex has made itself completely at home.

Two of the island's signature features are its near-perfect climate and its rugged, mountainous terrain, and the house takes full advantage of both. A stucco garden wall surrounds the property, enclosing a living environment that makes only the most casual distinc-tions between indoors and out. The central living space, a large dining area with a small kitchen alcove, is as much a porch as it is an enclosed room. With stout columns and broad, overhanging eaves but no exterior walls to speak of, it opens toward one of the island's many steep volcanic peaks on one side and the blue waters of St. Jean Bay on the other. "I've seen a rainbow start on one side and end on the other," Roosevelt says. "I've seen it raining on one side and not the other." Flanking the dining area, and offering a more indoor experience, are a large living room and a sleeping wing

Opposite—The same smooth terra cotta tiles that cover the patios run through the interior of the house, blurring the distinction between indoor and outdoor spaces. Rainwater that falls on the roof flows into cisterns in the exterior walls. Terra cotta spouts shed overflow away from the building. Above—The living room's vaulted brick ceiling conveys a sense of coolness and shelter.

Above left—The central kitchen and dining space is nearly as much a covered porch as it is an enclosed room. Above right—The bedroom wing is topped with a ladder-access study.

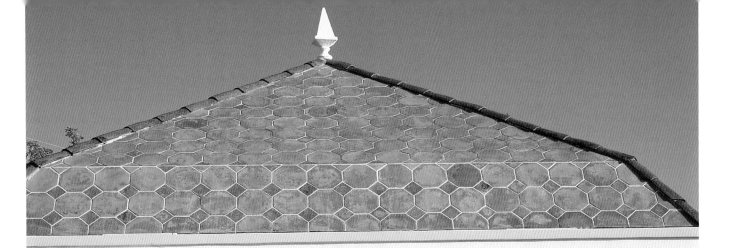

with two bedrooms and a ladder-access study loft. Vaulted brick ceilings and thick stuccoed walls reinforce the sense of shelter (terra cotta-tiled roofs channel rainwater to cisterns built into those walls, conserving a precious commodity and helping to cool the interior). But with their outward-hinging French doors, these rooms, too, open wide to the outdoors. Smooth terra cotta tiles lie underfoot everywhere, from the garden gate, through the house, to the pool deck, with its shady ajoupa and elevated views of the sea.

A life that flows effortlessly between indoors and out holds some surprises for the uninitiated, though.

Left—Mosquito nets protect against night-flying insects in a house where doors and windows tend to remain wide open. Above—Garden walls foster a sense of privacy and security without blocking some of the island's finest views.

"When it rains, if you don't close those hurricane doors, you have a flood," Roosevelt warns. Sleeping with windows flung open means waking "when the roosters start to crow and the sun comes up over the mountain." Hermit crabs wander through the house. At the table with friends one evening, "I felt something in my hair," she says, "and it was a tree frog." Instantly, the tiny creature sprang to another surprised head and then another, she laughs. "It made the rounds of the dinner party." Given the benign nature of the local fauna, though, and the island's salutary effect on its human residents, such uninvited guests are tolerated. That's the nature of St. Barth. And it is very much the nature of this house, says its owner. "It's a very warm, special, gracious space."

Robertson House

America's major homebuilders turn out tens of thousands of houses in a year. But after the warranty period expires, chances are that few owners will remember who built theirs. The houses Joseph Eichler built in California during the 1950s and 1960s so captured the feeling of their time and place that, even fifty years later, they still go by his name. Inspired by the architecture of Frank Lloyd Wright, Eichler made it his job to bring contemporary, open-plan living to the middle class. He succeeded to the tune of some 11,000 houses, most of them in and around San Francisco. Modest in size but long on style and designed for

Built in 1964 by the innovative homebuilder Joseph Eichler, this house shares design features with thousands of other Eichler homes in northern California. But its location on the shore of San Francisco Bay is anything but mass produced. At high tide, the building's full-width deck extends over the water. Its adjoining deep-water dock is large enough for an ocean-going yacht.

Opposite—The entry courtyard offers shelter from the wind and shade from the sun, but the see-through living room maintains its connection to the Bay. Above—Facing southwest, the house takes in views from the Sausalito waterfront to the Golden Gate Bridge.

California's mild climate, the houses have aged gracefully, and the current revival of interest in mid-century Modernism has only added to their cachet. Most Eichler homes were built in subdivisions, where the architecture had to generate its own drama. Pam and Jim Robertson's Eichler is another story. Smack on the shore of Belvedere Island, this 1964 Eichler has a deep-water dock on San Francisco Bay and a view that stretches from the Sausalito waterfront to the towers of the Golden Gate Bridge.

When the Robertsons first toured the house with their real-estate agent, though, they were less than impressed. A previous owner had gone overboard with the landscaping—"The front yard was loaded with boulders the size of cars," Jim Robertson says—and the worn interior, with its palette of browns and blacks, was even worse. "The first time we saw it we walked in and walked out." Only a tight housing market and their second-child's impending due date brought them back for another look. Two remodeled baths and a few cans

of paint later, they began to see what a gem they had on their hands.

"We thought we were fairly traditional," Robertson says. But after living here, "there are features of an Eichler home that I would never want to be without. The entry courtyard is perfect when the weather is tough—too windy or too sunny—and you can still enjoy the bay side, because there's so much glass." The continuum of courtyard, living room, and full-width deck make it "a free-flowing party house." In its simplicity and openness, the Eichler esthetic is still a breath of fresh air. "It encapsulates the California dream of yesteryear. When you walk in, you instantly hear music from that era; you hear Herb Alpert. It's a fun place to be."

The location doesn't hurt, either. "The key thing about the house," Robertson says, "is it's changing colors all the time, because it's facing southwest. From early fall through winter you get some of the most incredible sunsets. You get everything from deep pur-

Opposite and below—A bit of restrained interior design and two remodeled bathrooms were all it took to bring this mid-century Modern house up to date. More than 40 years after it was built, it embodies a 1960s California esthetic that appeals to far more than mere nostalgia.

Robertson House 187

ples to monochromatic gray-greens in the storms." The bay, which laps under the deck at high tide, is a window into another world. "Our kids' point of reference for wildlife is pelicans, sharks, rays, egrets. And then there are the seals. Some seasons, they bark all night, like dogs." The Robertsons keep a small powerboat on their dock, for trailing junior-class sailing races or putting over to the yacht club for dinner. But one can't look at all that saltwater without thinking bigger thoughts, Robertson says. "It's kind of interesting to know that you could leave your back door, and, if you had a big enough boat, there's nothing between you and Hawaii or Japan."

James House

Carmel, California
Charles Sumner Greene, architect

Greene & Greene is one of the enduring brand names of the Arts & Crafts movement. During the prime of their architecture practice, in the opening years of the 20th century, the brothers Charles and Henry Greene elevated the style to the realm of fine art, while remaining true to its ideals of craftsmanship and the honest expression of natural materials. The most elaborate of their wooden houses, now sometimes called the "ultimate bungalows," shaped an emerging California style of residential architecture whose influence quickly spread across the country. By the mid-1910s, though, Greene & Greene had passed its peak. Charles, the elder brother, left the firm's Pasadena office for the coastal town of Carmel and more contemplative pursuits.

There, Charles Greene's path took an unexpected turn. D.L. James, a wealthy Kansas City merchant, offered him the commission to design a vacation home

Above—Built between 1918 and 1922 as a vacation home for a Kansas City merchant, the James house conveys the somewhat fantastic image of a medieval citadel on the California shore. Opposite above—The softly modeled forms of the interior contrast with the rugged surfaces of the building's stone shell. Opposite below left—A recent renovation added a new wing framed in wood.

atop the shorefront cliffs of Carmel Highlands. James's site offered limitless potential, and his deep pockets would allow the architect to approach the project as artist and master builder as well. Greene accepted, and the resulting building, called Seaward, remains one of his most admired.

The Pasadena bungalows, on their comfortable suburban lots, are temples of wood, their long overhangs providing shelter from the southern California sun. Here, facing the fog and storms of the Pacific, Greene chose a very different idiom. Using granite from a nearby quarry, his masons fashioned massive walls that seem to grow out of the site, their exposed foundations filling voids in the bedrock as if they had

been laid by natural deposition rather than human hands. The walls thicken at the building's corners and openings, reinforcing the impression of immense weight. To create the illusion of age, Greene instructed his workers to chip the edges of the terra cotta roof tiles. The rugged arches and stone courtyards that spread outward from the house, and the tile-topped chimneys that rise above it, suggest the ruins of some impossibly earlier building, as if a medieval monastery had once stood on this western shore.

Inside, the house shows a gentler face, with curved plaster surfaces in muted colors and wooden floors, doors, and ceilings. In contrast with the rough, broken granite of the exterior walls, the marble used at the

Top—The new wing includes a bedroom with a connected green-house. Left and above—The original interior represents the work of an architect given free rein to craft even the smallest details.

Opposite—Built of granite from a nearby quarry, the house looks very much a part of the cliffs on which it stands. That impression of immovable mass is reassuring here, where precipitous drops and the surf's constant pounding announce that this truly is the edge of the continent.

interior is carved in soft, organic forms. The stern, mineral aspect that the building turns toward the weather makes the burnished warmth of the interior all the more soothing, but even here one feels the building's protective embrace. The walls' great thickness shows at the window returns, where, looking out on the magnificent surf-battered cliffs below, one might well appreciate that reassuring mass. Perched at the precipitous edge of the continent, this house seems as immovable as the cliffs to which it is rooted.

No building is impervious to the elements, however, and Seaward owes its present pristine condition to an exhaustive renovation initiated by its current owners. That recent work also included a substantial addition. Framed in wood, the new construction strays from Greene's formula but does nothing to diminish the power of his original work. This house is one for the ages.

Architectural Resources

Koehler House
Bay of Fundy, Canada

Julie Snow Architects
2400 Rand Tower
527 Marquette Avenue
Minneapolis, MN 55402
www.juliesnowarchitects.com

Island Retreat
Coastal Maine

Lance Grindle,
builder/designer
P.O. Box 201
Seal Cove, ME 04674
Tel. 207-244-7601

Summer Cottage
Sorrento, Maine

Bernhard & Priestly
Architecture
23 Central Street
Rockport, ME 04856
Tel. 207-236-7745
www.bp-architecture.com

Deer Isle House
Deer Isle, Maine

Elliott Elliott Norelius
Architecture
86 Main Street
Blue Hill, ME 04614
Tel. 207-374-2566

Burns/Spaulding House
Georgetown, Maine

Whitten Architects
37 Silver Street
Portland, ME 04112
Tel. 207-774-0111
www.whittenarchitects.com

Cavalli Beach House
Biddeford Pool, Maine

Myers & Yanko, architects
7704 Shirley Drive
St. Louis, MO 63105
314-872-3006

Nolen/Denny Vacation House
Cape Cod, MA

Breese Architects
11 Beech Street
Vineyard Haven, MA 02568
www.breesearchitects.com

Harper's Island House
Chatham, MA

Polhemus Savery DaSilva
Architects Builders
101 Depot Road
Chatham, MA 02633
Tel. 508-945-4500
www.psdab.com

Roach House
Nantucket, MA

McMillen Interior Design
and Decoration
155 East 56th Street
New York, NY 10022
Tel. 212-753-5600

Jeffers House
Martha's Vineyard, MA

Polshek Partnership
Architects
320 West 13th Street
New York, NY 10014
Tel. 212-807-7171
www.polshek.com

Two Cottages
Martha's Vineyard, MA

Hutker Architects
Tisbury Market Place
79 Beach Road
Vineyard Haven, MA 02568
Tel. 508-693-3344
www.hutkerarchitects.com

Writer's Cottage
Martha's Vineyard, MA

South Mountain Company
15 Red Arrow Road
West Tisbury, MA 02575
Tel. 508-693-4850

Vacation House
Rhode Island

Shope Reno Wharton
Architecture
18 West Putnam Avenue
Greenwich, CT 06830
Tel. 203-869-7250

McKenna House
Hilton Head, SC

Group 3 Architects
1600 Main Street
Hilton Head Island, SC
29926
Tel. 843-689-9060

Caribbean Vacation House
St. Barthelemy

BSSW Architects
1500 Jackson Street
Fort Meyers, FL 33901
Tel. 239-278-3838
www.bsswarchitects.com

Roosevelt House
St. Barthelemy

Miles Reinke, architect

Robertson House
Belvedere, California

Eichler Homes,
builder/developer

James House
Carmel, California

Charles Sumner Greene,
architect